How to Analyze the Music of

BOB
DYLAN

by Teresa Ryan Manzella

ABDO
Publishing Company

Essential Critiques

How to Analyze the Music of

BOB
DYLAN

Content Consultant: Claire Colebrook, PhD, professor,
Department of English, Pennsylvania State University

Credits

Published by ABDO Publishing Company, 8000 West 78th Street, Edina, Minnesota 55439. Copyright © 2012 by Abdo Consulting Group, Inc. International copyrights reserved in all countries. No part of this book may be reproduced in any form without written permission from the publisher. The Essential Library™ is a trademark and logo of ABDO Publishing Company.

Printed in the United States of America,
North Mankato, Minnesota
062011
092011

 THIS BOOK CONTAINS AT LEAST 10% RECYCLED MATERIALS.

Editor: Holly Saari
Copy Editor: Sarah Beckman
Interior Design and Production: Marie Tupy
Cover Design: Kazuko Collins

Library of Congress Cataloging-in-Publication Data
Manzella, Teresa Ryan.
  How to analyze the music of Bob Dylan / by Teresa Ryan Manzella.
     p. cm. -- (Essential critiques)
  Includes bibliographical references and index.
  ISBN 978-1-61783-090-7
  1. Dylan, Bob, 1941---Criticism and interpretation--Juvenile literature. 2.
Popular music--United States--History and criticism--Juvenile literature. I. Title.
  ML3930.D97M36 2012
  782.42164092--dc22
                                      2011006299

Table of Contents

Introduction to Critiques

What Is Critical Theory?

What do you usually do when you listen to music? You probably enjoy the different instruments you can hear. You also follow the melodies and harmonies and try to understand a song's lyrics. Yet these are only a few of many possible ways of understanding and appreciating music. What if you are interested in delving more deeply? You might want to learn more about the musician and how his or her personal background is reflected in the song. Or you might want to examine what the song says about society—how it depicts the roles of women and minorities, for example. If so, you have entered the realm of critical theory.

Critical theory helps you learn how various works of art, literature, music, theater, film, and

other endeavors either support or challenge the way society behaves. Critical theory is the evaluation and interpretation of a work using different philosophies, or schools of thought. Critical theory can be used to understand all types of cultural productions.

There are many different critical theories. If you are analyzing music, each theory asks you to look at the work from a different perspective. Some theories address social issues, while others focus on the musician's life, what role the song plays in the musician's collected songs, or the time period in which the song was written or set. For example, the critical theory that asks how a musician's life affected the music is called biographical criticism. Other common schools of criticism include historical criticism, feminist criticism, psychological criticism, and New Criticism, which examines a work solely within the context of the work itself.

What Is the Purpose of Critical Theory?

Critical theory can open your mind to new ways of thinking. It can help you evaluate music from a new perspective, directing your attention to issues and messages you may not otherwise recognize in a work. For example, applying feminist criticism to a song may make you aware of female stereotypes perpetuated in the work. Applying a critical theory to a work helps you learn about the person who created it or the society that enjoyed it. You can explore how the song is perceived by current cultures.

How Do You Apply Critical Theory?

You conduct a critique when you use a critical theory to examine and question a work. The theory you choose is a lens through which you can view the work, or a springboard for asking questions about the work. Applying a critical theory helps you think critically about the work. You are free to question the work and make an assertion about it. If you choose to examine a song using biographical theory, for example, you want to know how the songwriter's personal background or education inspired or shaped the work. You could explore why the musician was drawn to the subject. For instance, are there any parallels between the subject of the lyrics and the musician's life?

Forming a Thesis

Ask your question and find answers in the work or other related materials. Then you can create a thesis. The thesis is the key point in your critique. It is your argument about the work based on the tenets, or beliefs, of the theory you are using. For example, if you are using biographical theory to ask how the musician's life inspired the work, your thesis could be worded as follows: Musician Teng Xiong, raised in refugee camps in Southeast Asia, drew upon her experiences for her album *No Home for Me*.

> **How to Make a Thesis Statement**
>
> In a critique, a thesis statement typically appears at the end of the introductory paragraph. It is usually only one sentence long and states the author's main idea.

Providing Evidence

Once you have formed a thesis, you must provide evidence to support it. Evidence might take the form of examples and quotations from the work itself—such as lyrics from a song. Articles about the album or personal interviews with the musician might also support your ideas. You may wish to address what other critics have written about the work. Quotes from these individuals may help support your claim. If you find any quotes or examples that contradict your thesis, you will need to create an argument against them. For instance: <u>Many critics have pointed to the album *No Home for Me* as detailing only the powerless circumstances Xiong faced. However, in the song "My Destiny," Xiong clearly depicts herself as someone who can shape her own future.</u>

> ### How to Support a Thesis Statement
>
> A critique should include several arguments. Arguments support a thesis claim.
> An argument is one or two sentences long and is supported by evidence from the work being discussed.
>
> Organize the arguments into paragraphs. These paragraphs make up the body of the critique.

In This Book

In this book, you will read overviews of famous songs, albums, and musical periods of musician Bob Dylan, each followed by a critique. Each critique will use one theory and apply it to his work. Critical thinking sections will give you a chance to consider other theses and questions about the work. Did you agree with the author's application of the theory? What other questions are raised by the thesis and its arguments? You can also find out what other critics think about particular songs and albums. Then, in the You Critique It section in the final pages of this book, you will have an opportunity to create your own critique.

Look for the Guides

Throughout the chapters that analyze the works, thesis statements have been highlighted. The box next to the thesis helps explain what questions are being raised about the work. Supporting arguments have been underlined. The boxes next to the arguments help explain how these points support the thesis. Look for these guides throughout each critique.

Bob Dylan, then known as Robert Zimmerman, began playing music seriously when he moved to Minneapolis in 1959.

2

A Closer Look at Bob Dylan

Bob Dylan was born Robert Allan Zimmerman on May 24, 1941, in Duluth, Minnesota, as the older of two sons of first-generation Jewish Americans. When he was six years old, his family moved to Hibbing, Minnesota. He lived there until graduating from Hibbing High School in 1959.

Robert began playing the piano at a young age and then began playing the guitar when he was 16. His first public performance was in Hibbing in 1957. He played the piano in a school talent show with some friends who had formed a band called the Shadow Blasters. The music, in the style of Little Richard, surprised the audience. Most people in rural Minnesota were not used to hearing rock and roll at that time. Robert moved on to form a trio called the Golden Chords, and the group played at local restaurants in Hibbing during his remaining high school years.

The Start of a Musical Career

Zimmerman, as he was called then, moved to Minneapolis in September 1959 to attend the University of Minnesota. Although his career as a student did not last long, his career as a musician began that fall in Minneapolis. He established himself in the local folk-music scene and soon made his first recording of folk music. By 1960, he decided to move to New York City to further his career.

Many important musicians lived in New York City, including Zimmerman's idol, Woody Guthrie. He met Guthrie in January 1961, not long after arriving in New York. Among the influential artists he encountered later was Joan Baez, who would prove to be a central person in Zimmerman's life. She liked his music, and the two dated casually for some time. She also got other, more established performers, such as the top folk group Peter, Paul, and Mary, to sing Zimmerman's songs.

Baez is often credited with having helped launch Zimmerman's career.

In 1962, Zimmerman officially changed his name to Bob Dylan. That same year, he released his debut solo album, *Bob Dylan*. He was becoming prominent in the civil rights movement, and he performed at the 1963 March on Washington for Jobs and Freedom, where Martin Luther King Jr. delivered his "I Have a Dream" speech. Dylan's reputation was building, and he was invited to play at key music events, among them the Newport Folk Festival in Rhode Island.

The Scene Changes

Dylan was a major figure in the music world by the mid-1960s, and he toured in the United States and Europe. He began to change his music to incorporate electronic and amplified instruments around this time, which caused some controversy among his friends who played folk music. But Dylan knew that he needed to keep up with the times, and purely acoustic folk music was losing its audience to folk-rock groups. His success alienated him from some in the New York music scene around that time.

In 1965, Dylan married Sara Lownds. They were married for several years and had a family together, but they went through a bitter divorce in 1977. The relationship was the inspiration for a number of Dylan's songs.

In 1966, Dylan was in a motorcycle accident, an incident that is shrouded in mystery. Though not seriously injured, he canceled upcoming performances and bowed out of other music commitments he had made. Dylan biographer Howard Sounes wrote about this event: "In this way the first part of a remarkable career drew to a close."[1]

Slowing Down

After his accident, Dylan took a break from performing. He became somewhat secluded at his home in Woodstock, New York, and focused on writing and recording, using recording equipment installed in the basement of his home. He also began painting as another form of artistic expression. Although somewhat private during this time, he did partake in some public artistic actions and events. In 1967, he wrote "All Along the Watchtower," which was covered and made into a

chart-topping hit by Jimi Hendrix. He next appeared in public at a memorial tribute to Woody Guthrie in 1968. He even rejected requests to play at the

Dylan played with Johnny Cash on *The Johnny Cash Show* in 1969.

Woodstock Festival in 1969, though he did appear on Johnny Cash's television show that year.

In the early 1970s, Dylan became involved with the film industry following his move back to New York City. He wrote music for movies such as *Pat Garrett and Billy the Kid*, which was released in 1973. The film included the chart-topping song, "Knockin' on Heaven's Door," which has been covered numerous times.

On the Road to More Change

Eight years passed before Dylan toured again with his band, and though the years away from touring had been productive ones, he decided to return to a busy schedule of public performances. From 1974 through the end of the decade, he played venues all over the world, including in Australia and Japan. Dylan also released nine albums during this period, making it another highly prolific time for him.

The late 1970s were a time of change for a lot of performers who had engaged enthusiastically in the wild and experimental times of the preceding decade. Many of these people sought religion, including Dylan. Though he had been raised in the Jewish faith and had spent some earlier years revisiting his religious roots, he converted to Christianity in 1979. This change influenced his writing significantly, and his songs took on a distinctly religious feel for a time.

Dylan's career evolved over the next decade, moving away from touring with just his own band to collaborating with other artists. During the 1980s, he appeared with the Grateful Dead and Tom Petty. He performed at the 1985 Live Aid concert with Keith Richards. In 1988 and 1990, he released two

Dylan, *second from right,* performed with musicians George Harrison, Roger McGuinn, and Tom Petty for a 1993 television special.

albums with the Traveling Wilburys, a band that included Roy Orbison and George Harrison.

Elder Statesman of Music

As he aged, Dylan's touring slowed again, and he began to receive achievement awards for his work. In 1982, he was inducted into the Songwriters' Hall of Fame and in 1988, he was inducted into the Rock and Roll Hall of Fame. In the 1990s, he received more honors, including three 1998 Grammy Awards for his album *Time Out of Mind* (1997). Many of his early songs were rereleased on collections of greatest hits.

The twenty-first century has seen Dylan continue to tour, paint, and write. An award-winning movie, *I'm Not There* (2007), was inspired by his life and work. The remarkable Special Citation Pulitzer Prize was bestowed upon Dylan in 2008. This award was given to Dylan for the profound impact his work has had on US popular culture.

An influence to more than one generation of aspiring artists, Dylan was still creating and performing in 2011, with more than 50 albums released in his career. He continued a limited touring schedule, and his paintings were on display in European museums. Although his albums have never sold in the numbers seen by some other musicians of his era, tickets to his live performances still sell out.

Fans gravitated toward Dylan's protest music, which captured the emotions they were feeling.

3

An Overview of Dylan's Protest Songs

A number of Dylan's early songs were used by various groups who were intent on creating social change. Dylan seemed to have a gift for penning just the right lyrics at just the right times, a gift that helped propel him into the spotlight. His words struck a chord with Americans who were caught in a time of intense upheaval and who needed someone to express their feelings of uncertainty.

Quickly Written Protest Songs

Two songs in particular, "A Hard Rain's A-Gonna Fall" and "Blowin' In The Wind," were used in protest for social change. Each of these songs was composed in a very short amount of time in cafés near the Gaslight, a club in New York City where Dylan often performed. He furiously typed out the lyrics or wrote them on a notepad, ripped them out, and ran over to the Gaslight to sing the new songs. The chords were not completely finalized before he presented the new tunes to his audience, but he had them firmed up by the time he finished playing.

"A Hard Rain's A-Gonna Fall" depicts the world following nuclear war. Dylan was just old enough for the military draft, and he was terrified. His angst reflected the level of anxiety in the nation, and Dylan put it on paper. Howard Sounes wrote that Dylan later said, "Every line was the start of a song he did not think he would have time to write."[1] Yet the words flow together and sound as though they were all meant to be part of the same song.

"Blowin' In The Wind" is Dylan's arrangement of a traditional slave song called "No More Auction Block." He borrowed the latter's melody and meter outline, which is a common practice in folk music. The lyrics are Dylan's original words, however. "Blowin' In The Wind" asks relentless questions — about war, oppression, and how cruel humans can be — that cry out for change, again capturing the

zeitgeist of a world on the edge. However, Dylan did not want to be pigeonholed as a protest artist and stated the song was not a protest song. Still, "Blowin' In The Wind" was an instant success, often thought of as a protest song, and other artists began performing it almost immediately.

In addition to the guitar, Dylan also played the harmonica.

Purposeful Protest Song

Dylan wrote what would become another protest song, "The Times They Are A-Changin'," on his first trip to England. The song was on the album *The Times They Are A-Changin'*, which was released in 1964. Some of his musical colleagues believed the entire album demonstrated a leap in musical and lyrical development. They attributed his advances to influences he was exposed to overseas.

While most of Dylan's songs have been viewed as just flowing freely from his mind through a pen or a typewriter, this song seems to have more of a formula to its composition. Dylan said he wrote it in response to what people seemed to want to hear at the time. The lyrics express impatience with what was called the "establishment."

Indeed, "The Times They Are A-Changin'," like "A Hard Rain's A-Gonna Fall" and "Blowin' In The Wind" before it, was popular with groups that were looking for a piece that put to music what they were feeling. According to Dylan biographer Clinton Heylin, rebellious young people—as well as civil rights activists—adopted the tune, because they "considered it a song as much about the generation gap" as about politics.[2]

Songs Just Waiting to be Written Down

Dylan's ability to take the pulse of his surroundings and articulate what he found there made him very famous, very fast. He claimed that he had no special talent for writing lyrics, though. When asked about the sources of his inspiration for the words to these songs, he consistently said, "The songs are there. They exist all by themselves just waiting for someone to write them down."[3] History has shown that Dylan picked the right moments to write down these three songs. Not only did they speak to the sentiments of the 1960s, they still resonate with many people today.

Dylan was reluctant to call himself a protest artist.

4

How to Apply Social Criticism to Dylan's Protest Songs

What Is Social Criticism?

Social criticism is a form of criticism that focuses on the social and political events or debates that were occurring during the time in which the artist created his or her work. Critics examine a work in the context of the social climate the artist may have been interpreting in the piece or the conditions that may have led to the thoughts that inspired the work.

When analyzing a work using social criticism, an author may research information on events that were current at the time the piece was written, as well as the artist's social and political leanings. Then the author constructs arguments and justifications that incorporate all of these findings.

Applying Social Criticism to Dylan's Protest Songs

Dylan's earliest recorded songs captured the attention of music fans in the United States and around the world because they used poetic language in popular songs to speak of serious issues. Against a backdrop of the Cold War, the construction of the Berlin Wall, and the Cuban missile crisis abroad, civil rights struggles were brewing at home. The United States was also just beginning its involvement in South Vietnam. Many people were unsure about how these situations would be resolved. They felt frustrated as world leaders put people's lives on the line, and they found their feelings expressed in Dylan's music. In the early twenty-first century, some minority groups in the United States are still trying to attain full civil rights, and the nation is involved in political engagements and war on several fronts. Though "The Times They Are A-Changin'," "A Hard Rain's A-Gonna Fall," and

Thesis Statement

The thesis statement, or main idea, of the essay is presented: "Though 'The Times They Are A-Changin',' 'A Hard Rain's A-Gonna Fall,' and 'Blowin' In The Wind' were written in the early 1960s, the songs' themes of questioning the political status quo and calling for an end to oppression continue to apply to the contemporary social climate." The author will prove this thesis in the rest of the essay.

"Blowin' In The Wind" were written in the early 1960s, the songs' themes of questioning the political status quo and calling for an end to oppression continue to apply to the contemporary social climate.

Warning various groups mentioned in the lyrics that they must either adapt or get out of the way, "The Times They Are A-Changin'" questions the roles and practices of the politicians and critics who hold power in society. The song was written in 1963, when demonstrations against racial prejudice and discrimination took place and ensuing riots erupted. President John F. Kennedy had sent thousands of troops to Birmingham, Alabama, to quell the disturbances that erupted after the arrest of Martin Luther King Jr. People worried about their right of freedom of expression being violated. The singer chides writers and critics to "keep your eyes wide / The chance won't come again," hinting that society may sometimes not notice what they should about what is going on.[1] The singer also states many

> **Argument One**
> The author has begun to argue the thesis. The first main point is: "Warning various groups mentioned in the lyrics that they must either adapt or get out of the way, 'The Times They Are A-Changin' questions the roles and practices of the politicians and critics who hold power in society."

changes people will have to adapt to, saying, "The line it is drawn / The curse it is cast . . . The order is Rapidly fadin.'"[2] And he tells senators and congressmen, "Don't stand in the doorway / Don't block up the hall."[3] This let the politicians know they should not get in the way of the change people were rallying for. Many different groups were looking for shifts toward greater liberties, and they wanted elected leaders to help, not hinder, that process.

In addition to wanting better lives for themselves, the people who were working for change in the United States knew that societies all over the world needed to improve. "Blowin' In The Wind" demands to know how long the suffering caused by power-seeking world leaders must continue before people will take a stand to stop it. In 1961, the United Nations General Assembly issued a resolution condemning the practice of apartheid, the systematic segregation and oppression of black people in South Africa. But one year later, when "Blowin' In The Wind" was written, nothing had really changed in

> **Argument Two**
> The author now turns to the next argument in support of the thesis: "'Blowin' In The Wind' demands to know how long the suffering caused by power-seeking world leaders must go on before people will take a stand to stop it."

the country. People in South Africa and many other places in the world continued to live with ruthless leaders, and television had begun to bring the news of their plights into US living rooms every night. The singer asks many questions about war and liberty, about how a person in charge of a nation can ignore the citizens' suffering, and when it will end: "how many deaths will it take till he knows / That too many people have died?"[4] The questions bring attention to what happens when politicians try to gain more land or power. Because "the answer is blowin' in the wind," all people can hear it and take action to make things better.[5]

Dylan's lyrics are often complex, with many songs holding deeper meanings. The powerful symbolism in "A Hard Rain's A-Gonna Fall" is often understood as describing the state of the earth after nuclear war, the threat of which was on people's minds in the early 1960s. The Cuban missile crisis had left many Americans concerned about the nuclear arms

> **Argument Three**
> The third argument addresses symbolism used by the artist to get the message across: "The powerful symbolism in 'A Hard Rain's A-Gonna Fall' is often understood as describing the state of the earth after nuclear war, the threat of which was on people's minds in the early 1960s."

race and how close the Soviet Union could get to US soil. Few people trusted Soviet leader Nikita Khrushchev, and the Cold War made many people nervous and suspicious. People around the world worried about the very possible launch of nuclear bombs. Fewer than 20 years had passed since World War II ended, and many remembered the horrors of the atomic bombs that brought the war's end. Collectively, these concerns lent to a tense social climate in which to live. In "A Hard Rain's A-Gonna Fall," "dead oceans" and "pellets of poison" speak of a devastated earth.[6] "Where black is the color, where none is the number" represents the darkness and the elimination of the human race that would result from such a conflict.[7]

Dylan's protest songs use strong imagery to depict flaws in the social and political status quo, imagery that remains descriptive of today's global climate. In "Blowin' In The Wind," the metaphor of a dove exhausted and sleeping in the sand from trying to bring peace to the world is very

> **Argument Four**
>
> The author now turns to why these songs are still listened to: "Dylan's protest songs use strong imagery to depict flaws in the social and political status quo, imagery that remains descriptive and potent in today's global climate."

powerful. Change that will "shake your windows and rattle your walls," from "The Times They Are A-Changin'," is something people must heed even

The messages in Dylan's protest music are still applicable today.

today.[8] World peace remains an elusive goal, and advances in technology also bring new methods of destruction with each passing year. Dylan's imagery speaks to conditions through the ages and not just those that existed during the 1960s.

No lasting answers have been found to the questions in Dylan's protest songs. Though "A Hard Rain's A-Gonna Fall," "Blowin' In The Wind," and "The Times They Are A-Changin'" contain pointed criticism of political and social systems that existed decades ago, these songs suggest the timelessness of Dylan's compelling music that calls for change. Although today the situations and leaders are different, similar conditions of oppression and nuclear threats—and calls for change, even within political campaigns such as Barack Obama's 2008 presidential run—keep people listening to and hearing the messages in Dylan's music.

Conclusion

The last paragraph is the conclusion of the critique. It brings together all the writer's arguments and partially restates the thesis, which has been supported by the evidence in each argument.

Thinking Critically about Dylan's Protest Songs

Now it is your turn to assess the critique. Consider these questions:

1. The thesis in this critique states that Dylan's protest songs remain relevant in today's social climate. Do you agree? Why or why not?

2. What was the strongest argument made? The weakest? Were the arguments supported with enough examples from the lyrics?

3. Do you think the conclusion does a good job of tying all of the arguments and the thesis statement together? Why or why not?

Other Approaches

What you have just read is one possible way to interpret Dylan's songs using social criticism. Are there other ways to apply social criticism to his works? Keep in mind that this type of criticism looks at a work within the context of the political and social climate that existed at the time the work was created. Two other approaches that could be used for a social critique follow. The first questions whether Dylan is involved deeply enough in politics to write songs he truly means. The second takes the approach that Dylan's words are not true poetry intended to create social change.

Dylan Was Apolitical

One way to write a criticism is to argue against another writer's thesis. The arguments that came before supported a thesis that assumed Dylan had strong feelings about social and political events that were happening around the time he was writing the songs discussed. A critic could take a completely different view. The thesis statement for such an approach might be: Though Dylan is often seen as a spokesman for the US counterculture, he has never been active politically or concerned about politics at all; therefore, his songs cannot be political protests calling for social change.

Rhetoric, Not Cultural Poetry

Not everyone who listens to Dylan's words thinks he has produced serious poetry about important social events. Some think he is just being preachy and that he has been lucky the words come together as well as they do. A thesis statement for this approach might be: Although Dylan's lyrics are widely read as deeply focused poetry composed to address serious issues of his time, Dylan's purpose has been simply to complain, not to create social change.

Dylan could also play the piano.

An Overview of Dylan's Personal Songs

By the mid-1960s, Dylan was an
established star. Much of his fame
came from songs he wrote in the spirit
of protest, songs with which he and
numerous other artists had found great
popular success. Because he resisted
being confined to one category of
music and was going through changes that often
result from a rapid rise to stardom, his songs from
this time took on a more personal tone. He wrote
about his relationships: romantic ones, those with
other musicians, and those with his increasingly
demanding fans. These personal songs invite a broad
range of interpretation, though some of the lyrics are
very clearly directed at certain people or groups that
were important in Dylan's life at the time.

Dylan began dating Suze Rotolo in 1961.

"It Ain't Me, Babe"

Written in 1964, "It Ain't Me, Babe" from the album *Another Side of Bob Dylan* (1964) tells the story of a person who does not want to be confined to the restrictions of relationships. Dylan's breakup with Suze Rotolo around that time was difficult for him, even though he had not been faithful to her. Also, Dylan was feeling the demands of his growing audience were both gratifying and overwhelming; fan hysteria was becoming a fact of life for him. Dylan's relationship discussed in the song, whether with Rotolo or his fans, seems to vary depending on what line of the song is studied.

What is known is that this song, along with "Mr. Tambourine Man" written around the same time, ushered in a new style of writing for Dylan. Overt protest lyrics and folksy ballads were gone, replaced by songs that reflected what biographer Clinton Heylin called the "culture of his day."[1] Some critics have speculated that Dylan had begun experimenting with hallucinogenic drugs and that his songs from this period were influenced by those experiences. Others have suggested that Dylan had recently started appreciating the music of the Beatles, and the line "No, no, no, it ain't me, babe" from the chorus of "It Ain't Me, Babe" was a reference to the Beatles' song "She Loves You."[2] In any case, the song was very successful for Dylan and added to the momentum of his career.

Dylan's music captured audiences around the country.

"Positively 4th Street"

Dylan wrote "Positively 4th Street," released on *Bob Dylan's Greatest Hits* (1967), in 1965, shortly after he upended the Newport Folk Festival by performing with electric, amplified instruments. The song is Dylan's reaction to the way he was treated by the traditional folk musicians at and after that event.

This song is somewhat unusual. None of the lines—out of 12 verses—includes the words of the song title or direct indications of the song's meaning. Because of the circumstances surrounding its composition, biographer Howard Sounes wrote that "Positively 4th Street" stood for Dylan's assessment of his former New York friends, who were "not second or even third rate," but positively "*fourth*" rate.[3] Such a judgment of musicians Dylan had worked with in the folk-music community might seem harsh. However, Dylan's wild success had alienated many of these people, whose success was slim compared to Dylan's, and they acted out against him by talking negatively about him and excluding him from their performances. He responded, and the result was a song that sent an unmistakable message.

Though the release of this song followed shortly after "Like a Rolling Stone," which rose to Number 2 on the *Billboard* popularity chart, "Positively 4th Street" did not have the same level of success, only making it to the Number 7 position. "Like a Rolling Stone" has longer verses, a chorus, and more melodic variance, which may have accounted for its higher popularity. However,

Dylan received criticism for playing electric instruments, which did not produce the core sound of folk music.

"Positively 4th Street" captures the impact of a critical turning point in Dylan's career and working relationships, when he transitioned from acoustic to electric instruments and was rebuked by traditional folk musicians who had been his colleagues.

Selling Out or Growing Musically?

Dylan had established his career initially in the acoustic folk-music genre. When folk music began to evolve into folk-rock, it was natural for Dylan to evolve his music as well. His move away from writing protest songs and ballads to composing more personal songs did not cause an uproar, but he did cause an uproar by using amplification typical of rock and roll. Some people accused Dylan of selling out to achieve more commercial success, but musicians who produced less-edgy covers of his songs actually sold many more albums. The changes were a part of Dylan's musical development, happening in the context of his times.

Many of Dylan's songs reflect aspects of his personal life.

How to Apply Biographical Criticism to Dylan's Personal Songs

What Is Biographical Criticism?

Biographical criticism is a form of criticism that analyzes an artist's work based on knowledge of the artist's personal life. People create works of art, literature, and musical compositions, and their works are often impacted by aspects of their lives. Learning about details from an artist's personal life is an essential aspect of applying biographical criticism. The focus in this type of criticism is on examining how personal events and developments may have inspired a work's creation. The content of the piece is then interpreted with that background in mind.

As is the case for historical and social criticism, meaning in biographical criticism is contextual. In order to correctly assess and analyze the piece in question, a critic must do research into the relationships, living situation, professional successes and failures, even health issues that were in play when the artist wrote it. Also important are the systems of meaning that were available to the artist at the time. Systems of meaning are the ways in which a society or culture attaches meaning to certain things such as words, phrases, behaviors, and symbols. Once that research has been done, the critic explores ways to relate the information gathered about the artist to the work being critiqued.

Applying Biographical Criticism to Dylan's Personal Songs

Dylan was becoming very famous by 1964, when he began writing songs that were more about himself and his own life than about events in the world around him. His rapid rise to stardom had made him popular with women and a favorite among music fans in the cities he performed in. While he enjoyed the attention, he did not always enjoy having to deal with the demands people placed on him. His girlfriend Suze Rotolo, who he had dated since 1961, broke up with him in 1964 because he would not stop seeing other women. Fans adored him and would surround his taxi when he left performances, making it difficult for him to get away. He heard the music of the Beatles and began experimenting with electric guitars. His songs from this time reflect the personal changes and challenges he was going through. "It Ain't Me, Babe" and "Positively 4th Street" reveal Dylan's conflicting feelings about his relationships with people: he wanted to get what he desired and needed from others, but he did not want to live up to anyone else's requirements.

Dylan and Rotolo had known each other for around three years when he wrote "It Ain't Me, Babe." He traveled a great deal, playing in different places and meeting different women along the way. Dylan was fairly possessive of Rotolo, but he wanted to remain free and have his own space. Each verse of "It Ain't Me, Babe" begins by Dylan telling his lover to "Go" and continues with "'way, lightly,

Thesis Statement

The main idea of the essay is presented here: "'It Ain't Me, Babe' and 'Positively 4th Street' reveal Dylan's conflicting feelings about his relationships with people: he wanted to get what he desired and needed from others, but he did not want to live up to anyone else's requirements." The rest of the essay will prove this thesis.

Argument One

The author presents the first argument: "Each verse of 'It Ain't Me, Babe' begins by Dylan telling his lover to 'Go' and continues with "'way, lightly, melt back,' instructing her to leave him alone."

melt back," instructing her to leave him alone.[1] Any personal connections he made had to happen on his own terms, and he wanted to be able to send someone away when it suited him. Though most often interpreted as relating to Rotolo, this song has also been read as pertaining to his fans, who were becoming increasingly demanding of his time and energy. Dylan did not want to be the one "Who will promise never to part," nor did he wish to be "Never weak but always strong" for Rotolo or his audience.[2]

Argument Two

The author continues to argue the thesis: "Citing expectations that often exist in relationships, 'It Ain't Me, Babe' sends a clear message that Dylan will not meet those expectations."

When people are close, they usually assume a certain level of trust, reliability, and faithfulness. Citing expectations that often exist in relationships, "It Ain't Me, Babe" sends a clear message that Dylan will not meet those expectations. The lyrics exaggerate what people typically want from each other, especially "To protect you an' defend you / Whether you are right or wrong" and "Someone who will die for you an' more."[3] Dylan admitted, "I will only let you down."[4] He was not capable of being faithful or depended upon, and instead of trying to change that, he dismissed those who sought him out, stating, "It ain't me you're lookin' for, babe."[5] He most likely did not want his fans to get the impression that he planned to let them down, but he was fairly open about not being there for a girlfriend.

Dylan established his career as a musician by networking with folk musicians in New York City. Many of them had helped him get work and find places to stay. When he began introducing electric, amplified instruments into his performances, those same people reacted very negatively to the changes he was making. Written following time Dylan spent in the Greenwich Village folk-music scene, "Positively 4th Street" communicates his sense of betrayal caused by other musicians. Some folk musicians were purists who felt that only acoustic instruments should be used in folk music, and Dylan had violated that unwritten rule. After the Newport Folk Festival of 1965, he was no longer welcome among many of

> **Argument Three**
> Addressing the other song being analyzed, the author states: "Written following time Dylan spent in the Greenwich Village folk-music scene, 'Positively 4th Street' communicates his sense of betrayal caused by other musicians."

these performers. Lyrics such as "You got a lotta nerve / To say you are my friend" and "You say I let you down / You know it's not like that" speak to the changes in attitudes that he encountered.[6] People he had considered friends suddenly seemed disloyal.

Dylan's success also had the effect of alienating some artist friends he had worked with, because they were not achieving the same level of stardom he had attained. Later verses address the bitterness he experienced, which was triggered by getting rejected and feeling like an outsider. Accusing former friends of talking behind his back, the lyrics continue, "I used to be among the crowd you're in with."[7] Dylan knew he had been excluded, and he had ideas why this happened. The verse, "And now I know you're dissatisfied / With your position and your place / Don't you understand / It's not my problem," reveals that he picked up on their sense of failure, but he was too focused on his own rejection by these former friends to reach out and be compassionate.[8] The song was intended as an insult, and he ended it with a direct put-down, mentioning

> **Argument Four**
> The author presents the final argument: "Later verses address the bitterness he experienced, which was triggered by getting rejected and feeling like an outsider."

Some of Dylan's songs aimed pointed criticisms at those who had turned their backs on him.

if he changed places with the subject of his insults, "You'd know what a drag it is to see you."[9]

In New York, Dylan had a reputation as a person who would take what he needed from other people. He feels free to distance himself from a

Conclusion

The author summarizes the preceding arguments, revisits the ideas of the thesis statement, and closes the essay.

woman who wants to be in a close relationship with him in "It Ain't Me, Babe," yet he is bitter about receiving similar treatment from others he thought were friends, as reflected in "Positively 4th Street." Even though he benefited from others' generosity and wanted those he knew to be supportive of him, Dylan often did not reciprocate. The autobiographical songs he wrote during the mid-1960s provide powerful insight into his contradictory beliefs about relationships.

Thinking Critically about Dylan's Personal Songs

Now it is your turn to assess the critique. Consider these questions:

1. The thesis in this critique states that Dylan's personal songs reflect an inner conflict about making commitments to people in his life. Do you agree? Why or why not?

2. What was the strongest argument made? The weakest? Were the arguments supported with examples from the lyrics?

3. Would one of the other approaches on the next two pages make an easier or more effective thesis to argue about Dylan's personal songs? If so, how would you begin to argue that thesis? If not, why not?

Other Approaches

What you have just read is one potential way to interpret Dylan's personal songs using biographical criticism. Could there be other ways to apply biographical criticism to his works? Keep in mind that this type of criticism looks at a piece in the context of what was happening in the artist's life at the time the work was created. What come next are two other approaches that could be used for a biographical critique. The first maintains that Dylan was insecure about being able to live up to others' images of him rather than unwilling to do so. The second suggests Dylan was struggling with all of the changes that were happening in his life and that he was not ready for the fame he had found.

Dylan Was Insecure

This approach is not in direct conflict with the thesis that came before, but it interprets Dylan's motives differently. Such a difference in motivation can create a more positive or negative reflection on the subject of a biographical critique. A possible thesis statement for this approach might be: Though the lyrics from "It Ain't Me, Babe" and "Positively 4th Street" are often viewed as indicating Dylan did not wish to be subjected to anyone's expectations, they actually reflect his insecurities about being able to meet those expectations.

Too Much Change Too Fast

Some people who read the story of Dylan's rise to fame might wonder how so many significant changes happening so quickly might affect a person. A critic who focuses on this issue could engender sympathy for the target of the critique. The thesis statement for this tactic could be: Some have read the words from "It Ain't Me, Babe" and "Positively 4th Street" as indicators of Dylan's fickle nature; however, they are essentially gauges of the difficulties he was going through in trying to adjust to the rigors of his newfound fame.

Blood on the Tracks includes songs detailing matters of
Dylan's personal life.

An Overview of
Blood on the Tracks

In 1975, Dylan released his eighteenth album, *Blood on the Tracks*. This was an unusual album for him, in that the lyrics he wrote for it exposed his personal relationships in some detail. Unlike "Positively 4th Street" and "It Ain't Me, Babe," which also explored Dylan's personal relationships, these songs are about fairly specific people and places. The words fanned speculation about the state of his marriage to Sara Lownds, and the structures of the songs created snapshots of his life at the time the album was released.

Summer in Minnesota

In early 1974, Dylan purchased land with an old farmhouse on it, just a few miles northwest of Minneapolis. He spent the summer of 1974 on the farm, which was near his brother and mother, who both lived in Minneapolis. Dylan's wife, Sara, did not accompany him, but their children did. The couple's relationship was deteriorating by this time, and he had a girlfriend, Ellen Bernstein, who stayed with him in Minnesota. With his family near, he spent the summer relaxing on the farm and enjoying a tranquil respite from New York. Dylan converted the farmhouse into a home for his family, and he made the barn into an art studio. It was in this setting that the material for *Blood on the Tracks* was written: Dylan wrote 12 songs, ten of which made the final version of the album.

Songs like Paintings

During his time in Minnesota, Dylan was increasingly serious about his painting, and the techniques he was learning in his visual art came into play as he wrote his songs. Paintings often tell various parts of a story simultaneously, and Dylan set out to construct songs that did the same thing.

Dylan created a nonlinear storytelling method for some of the songs on *Blood on the Tracks.*

"Tangled Up in Blue," the first song on the album, represents Dylan's most successful effort to tell a story from a number of temporal perspectives. The lovers meet, share a relationship, and the narrator reflects on that relationship, but the progression in the lyrics is not linear. Dylan combined the different stages within the verses. He said, "I wanted to defy time, so that the story took place in the present and the past at the same time. I wanted that song to be like a painting."[1] "Simple Twist of Fate" is another song on the album constructed in this manner, which was a Dylan innovation.

Recording Challenges

Blood on the Tracks turned out to be a difficult album to record. After returning to New York, Dylan began recording at Columbia's studios in the fall of 1974, but he was not satisfied with the results. He brought in different backup players for various takes, but the outcomes fell short of what he sought to create. There was a feeling he wanted to capture with this album, and he was not getting it right in New York.

Dylan's brother, David, was a musician and sound technician in Minnesota. He worked at Sound 80 Studios, a facility in Minneapolis that many musicians highly regarded. Dylan went there in late 1974 to rerecord some of the tracks with players David knew to try to capture the right mood. Recording sessions went well, and the result was one of Dylan's most acclaimed and popular albums—considered by many listeners to be his personal best up to that point.

The Women in His Life

Though some of the songs on *Blood on the Tracks* are known to refer to Sara, she is not the only woman represented there. Dylan wrote and sang about Suze Rotolo and Ellen Bernstein, too, and many of the songs lament relationships between men and women in general. Dylan himself has wondered why an album so full of pain would be enjoyed so much by his fans.

The themes that run through these songs not only paint pictures of events in nonlinear ways, they also discuss the women in Dylan's life—and there had been several by then—in somewhat unflattering terms. The lyrics lend themselves to being interpreted as holding women as a gender responsible for much of the suffering in men's lives. Pain, loneliness, separation, and infidelity: according to this collection of songs, these are just a few of the problems women can cause for men. Dylan's first marriage ended not long after the completion of this album.

Dylan's "Tangled Up in Blue," "Idiot Wind," "You're Gonna Make Me Lonesome When You Go," and "If You See Her, Say Hello" from *Blood on the Tracks* depict women in negative ways.

How to Apply Feminist Criticism to *Blood on the Tracks*

What Is Feminist Criticism?

Feminist criticism is a form of criticism that derives significance from the gender of the creator of and the characters in a work. Focusing on how a piece treats women, a critic will analyze whether society's stereotypes are supported or opposed within the work. An author will look for symbolism to examine whether women are represented in positive or negative ways.

Feminist criticism also assumes that a piece is shaped by how it is read. Because women and men write and read from different perspectives, readers who plan to apply feminist criticism are encouraged to imagine themselves reading from the point of view of a woman. This may sound like it would be easy for female readers. However, women have typically been taught to read like men and to discount their own gender in many situations. Therefore, all readers must intentionally center on their feminine sides in order to be able to engage in effective feminist criticism.

Applying Feminist Criticism to *Blood on the Tracks*

Women have played a significant role in Dylan's life and work. Whether as a girlfriend, wife, supporter, or muse, there has almost always been at least one woman influencing his songs. Many of his songs, including "Tangled Up in Blue," "Idiot Wind," "You're Gonna Make Me Lonesome When You Go," and "If You See Her, Say Hello" from *Blood on the Tracks*, discuss women and aspects of their lives in ways that create images of women as creatures of narrow possibilities. Most of these depictions are limiting and do not afford women much personal value. Several songs on Dylan's album *Blood on the Tracks* reinforce stereotypes of women as unpredictable and unsubstantial.

Thesis Statement

The main idea of the essay is presented here: "Several songs on Dylan's album *Blood on the Tracks* reinforce stereotypes of women as unpredictable and unsubstantial." The author proves this thesis in the rest of the essay.

When a man and a woman enter into a romantic
relationship, they often trust each other and depend
on the other's reliability; yet,
based on Dylan's lyrics, Dylan
does not seem to count on these
aspects of a relationship. <u>The
chance meetings with and the
departures of women in "Tangled
Up in Blue" and "If You See
Her, Say Hello" depict women
as unstable relationship partners
who cannot be depended upon.</u>
In the first song, one woman was already married,
and she met the male singer when, "I helped her
out of a jam, I guess," and another woman was an
exotic dancer who approached the singer and "Said
to me, 'Don't I know your name?'"[1] In Dylan's
world, women were being unfaithful or engaged in
questionable enterprises when they came into his
life. And they left without provocation, as in "If You
See Her, Say Hello," where the lyrics state, "We had
a falling-out, like lovers often will / And to think of
how she left that night, it still brings me a chill."[2]
Dylan thought they just had a quarrel and that the
two were still in a relationship, but the woman

> **Argument One**
> The author introduces the
> first argument: "The chance
> meetings with and the
> departures of women in
> 'Tangled Up in Blue' and
> 'If You See Her, Say Hello'
> depict women as unstable
> relationship partners who
> cannot be depended upon."

left him permanently, showing Dylan she was not committed to making the relationship work.

Scattered throughout the songs are mentions of a lover's hair color, what her skin was like, and whether she was married, but little attention is given to her worth as a person. <u>By referring to women in the songs in terms of their appearance, body parts, status as men's wives, and work in the sexual entertainment business, many of the lyrics in *Blood on the Tracks* treat women as objects.</u> In "Tangled Up in Blue," Dylan writes, "She was married when we first met / Soon to be divorced," about one woman and mentions that others he knew "are carpenters' wives."[3] In "Idiot Wind," he writes that he took another man's "wife to Italy / She inherited a million bucks and when she died it came to me," hinting that these women did not have lives separate from their relationships with men.[4] Even what women did for work, if he brought it up, was about men: "She was workin' in a topless place," as he writes in "Tangled

> **Argument Two**
> Continuing to argue the thesis, the author states: "By referring to the women in the songs in terms of their appearance, body parts, status as men's wives, and work in the sexual entertainment business, many of the lyrics in *Blood on the Tracks* treat women as objects."

Up in Blue."[5] These references combine to create descriptions of women as objects that can be taken and used for enjoyment.

In "You're Gonna Make Me Lonesome When You Go," the singer expects his lover to leave him in emotional pain, as he believes most women leave men. The lyrics speak of the strongest love Dylan has experienced. He writes, "I've seen love go by my door / It's never been this close before," but every verse ends with the singer's broken heart: "Yer gonna make me lonesome when you go."[6] It is as if he could foresee, because "Situations have ended sad / Relationships have all been bad," that this relationship will be no different.[7] The lyrics refer to Verlaine and Rimbaud, two French poets and lovers whose stormy relationship ended when one shot the other in the hand, and imply that Dylan expected his affairs to run similar courses, though maybe without the violence. Sadness, bad endings, and loneliness were what he expected from the women in his life. He did not necessarily know when he would be abandoned, but that it was only a matter of time.

> **Argument Three**
> The third argument is now presented: "In 'You're Gonna Make Me Lonesome When You Go,' the singer expects his lover to leave him in emotional pain, as he believes most women leave men."

Dylan's writing for this album included the ability to be very sarcastic and sometimes downright cruel toward women. In "Idiot Wind," the singer refers to a former lover as an idiot and questions how she can function, being as unintelligent as she is. This song continually mentions an "Idiot wind, blowing every time you move your teeth," indicating that all of the words the woman speaks are senseless.[8] The song repeats, "You're an idiot, babe / It's a wonder that you still know how to breathe."[9] The singer implies the woman is so stupid she is barely alive, since breathing is a bodily function that she cannot control. Clearly, the male singer did not respect the intelligence of his former lover.

Although Dylan was known to spend a great deal of time in the company of women, he did not view them as equals. "Tangled Up in Blue," "Idiot Wind," "You're Gonna Make Me Lonesome When You Go," and

> **Argument Four**
> The last argument is now offered: "In 'Idiot Wind,' the singer refers to a former lover as an idiot and questions how she can function, being as unintelligent as she is."

> **Conclusion**
> Here, the author draws together the preceding arguments and supporting evidence, partially paraphrasing the thesis statement, to conclude the essay.

"If You See Her, Say Hello," from the album *Blood on the Tracks*, portray relationships with women as risky and painful, and they depict women as unreliable, unintelligent objects. Dylan portrays the

Although Dylan was often in a relationship with a woman, some of his songs assert he did not consider women his equals.

women in these songs, valued only for their looks, as unintelligent, unfaithful objects that are not the equals of men.

Thinking Critically about *Blood on the Tracks*

Now it is your turn to assess the critique.
Consider these questions:

1. The thesis in this critique states that the songs from *Blood on the Tracks* reinforce negative stereotypes about women. Do you agree? Why or why not?

2. Select one of the arguments and see if you can support it using a different song or two from the album. Does the argument still work?

3. Do you think the conclusion unites the arguments with the thesis statement effectively? Why or why not?

Other Approaches

What you have just read is one possible way
to interpret Dylan's *Blood on the Tracks* using
feminist criticism. Can you think of other ways to
apply feminist criticism to this work? Remember
that a feminist critic analyzes a work based on the
perspective of the reader's gender, the genders
of the artist and characters, and the approach to
gender stereotypes in a piece. What follow are two
other approaches that could be used for a feminist
critique. The first suggests Dylan was struggling to
work through the breakup of his marriage, and his
words express emotional pain. The second argues
Dylan was writing about women in ways that
shifted the blame for failed relationships—a blame
that was typically his—to women he had actually
wronged.

Dylan Was Heartbroken

The preceding essay contends the songs on
Blood on the Tracks are purposefully denigrating
to women because they support the stereotype of
women as men's accessories. Another author could
make the argument that Dylan was not thinking
about gender stereotypes when he wrote these
songs; rather, he was just in pain from his marriage

ending. Instead of hiding this emotional pain, he articulated it. A possible thesis statement for such an argument might be: Although some have read the lyrics to Dylan's *Blood on the Tracks* as reinforcing negative stereotypes of women, the words actually reflect Dylan's feminine side by expressing his heartbreak over failed relationships.

Unwilling to Admit Responsibility

Another potential way to view *Blood on the Tracks* from a feminist perspective is to argue Dylan was chronically unfaithful to the women in his life, but he was unwilling to face that fact. In order to prevent being held accountable for his actions toward women, he altered reality to show he was the injured party. The thesis statement for this approach might be: By writing lyrics that blamed the women in his life for his failed relationships, Dylan used the songs on *Blood on the Tracks* to deny his own unfaithfulness and irresponsibility that had led to those failures and to depict himself as an injured hero.

Some songs on Dylan's *Desire*, released in 1976, tell stories based on real events.

9

An Overview of "Hurricane" and "Joey" from *Desire*

In 1976, Dylan released the album *Desire*. By this time, he had moved far beyond the boundaries of folk and protest songwriting and singing. However, "Hurricane" and "Joey" tell stories of events that took place during the 1960s in a folk-music manner, which recall the music for which Dylan first received acclaim.

Collaborative Effort

Prior to the release of *Desire*, Dylan had only worked with other composers on two published songs. For *Desire*, Dylan worked with songwriter and stage director Jacques Levy on seven of the nine songs on the album, including "Hurricane" and "Joey." The two began working together after Dylan played Levy's material for Dylan's song "Isis," which was released on *Desire* in 1975. Levy was able to assist with tying thoughts together. Dylan had only begun learning how to write intentionally; for much of his career, he waited for inspiration and jotted down what came into his head. Levy had long been a more disciplined writer, so their styles complemented each other. Levy also introduced him to tools of the writer's trade that were unknown to Dylan—the thesaurus and the rhyming dictionary—which amazed Dylan with their usefulness.

Backstory of "Hurricane"

Rubin "Hurricane" Carter, a former middleweight boxer known for his quickness in the ring and his temper, was a young African-American man who had already amassed a long history of encounters with the criminal justice system when he was arrested for and convicted of a triple murder in 1966. The quality of the evidence against him was not strong, but eyewitnesses—who later confessed to being compensated for their testimony and lying under oath—placed him at the scene.

After being released from prison in 1988, Rubin Carter went on to advocate for those who had been wrongfully convicted.

Carter had served nearly eight years of the four life terms of his sentence when Viking Press published his autobiography, *The Sixteenth Round: From Number 1 Contender to #45472*. Dylan was among the celebrities to receive a copy of the book from Carter, and the man's story inspired Dylan to visit him in prison and to write the song "Hurricane." Dylan was able to condense a very complicated story into 11 verses sung in eight minutes, and Levy applied his theater background to add a dramatic quality to the song. Dylan performed "Hurricane" at every opportunity as he toured following the release of *Desire*.

The case eventually received sufficient attention to raise the funds required to mount a series of appeals. Though he had to endure 22 years in jail and multiple court decisions, Carter was ultimately cleared and freed from prison in 1988. Some sources have argued that he truly was guilty of the crime, but the judge who gave him his freedom stated racism had played a greater role than reason in his conviction.

Backstory of "Joey"

Although infamous for spreading violence and crime, gangsters and the mobs they belong to have long been favorite topics in US popular culture. The subject of Dylan's song "Joey" is a New York mobster named Joseph Gallo. He came from a family of active gangsters who were powerful in the President Street docks area of Brooklyn, New York.

Gallo had a reputation for being mean and violent, which is not reflected in the lyrics of "Joey." In fact, according to biographer Clinton Heylin, Dylan received "some pointed criticism in the press about a song that only appeared to glorify a vicious hoodlum."[1] Perhaps Dylan was attempting to emphasize the gentler side that Joey Gallo had tried to cultivate. In any case, the song has its own musical and lyrical qualities, regardless of how close it may be to the truth. Using acoustic instruments such as the mandolin and violin and a verse-chorus construction, Dylan created a piece that sounds almost like an Italian folk song. These features help it stand as an artistic work, even if it might not stand as an accurate piece of history.

Producing the Album

Dylan brought a large number of musicians to the studio to record *Desire*. More than 20 players of a variety of instruments, including accordion and violin, took part in the first day of recording. Unfortunately, this assemblage did not create the sound Dylan wanted to achieve. Several days, significantly fewer musicians, and numerous takes later, he was finally satisfied. *Desire* was completed just a few months after *Blood on the Tracks* was released, and it soon became a solid follow-up to that recording.

In 1975, Dylan performed a benefit concert to help Rubin Carter receive a new trial.

10

How to Apply Historical Criticism to "Hurricane" and "Joey" from *Desire*

What Is Historical Criticism?

Historical criticism analyzes a work through the lens of the work's historical context. This means the critic examines the historical mood and events during the time the work was created. As with social criticism, the meaning of a work analyzed using historical criticism is contextual, so it is important to understand the era of composition as well as the era from which the story is being told. When examining songs using historical criticism, an author may research information on world events occurring around the time the songs were composed. Also, changes that may have been taking place in society, technology, and ideas of the time can provide the background necessary to interpret the lyrics.

Applying Historical Criticism to "Hurricane" and "Joey" from *Desire*

Many exciting and positive changes were taking place in US culture during the 1960s, but some negative aspects of society still existed. The population was growing, and more people owned cars and homes than ever before, but not everyone who wanted to work had a job. Major civil rights legislation was enacted in 1964, but attitudes toward and treatment of African Americans did not change instantly with the new laws. Racially motivated crimes, though banned by the law, did not stop. Gangster violence continued to be a fact of life in large cities, and mob involvement substituted for an actual job for some people. Not everyone trusted the criminal justice system to dispense justice. Dylan was aware of these inequities and wrote about them in his music. "Hurricane" and "Joey" reflect concerns about the violence resulting from injustice and racism that were widespread in US society in the 1960s.

Thesis Statement

The author presents the thesis statement: "'Hurricane' and 'Joey,' written about the turbulent 1960s, reflect concerns about the violence resulting from injustice and racism that were widespread in US society at the time." The following paragraphs will prove the thesis.

In 1966, a triple murder took place in a New Jersey bar, and a white witness said he saw two African-American men leave the scene in a white car. Those two small pieces of information were enough to ruin a man's life. "Hurricane" tells a story of the unjust treatment of an African-American man at the hands of the police, the courts, and the media, who punished him for a crime he did not commit. Rubin "Hurricane" Carter was arrested, along with an alleged accomplice, tried, and convicted of killing three people. As Dylan wrote in the song, he was "the man the authorities came to blame / For somethin' that he never done."[1] The police in Carter's town disliked him. The police, according to the lyrics, persuaded a couple of petty criminals to help them create evidence. The song even speculates that the pair committed the murders. During the trial, these witnesses lied, the judge made Carter's own witnesses look bad, "and the newspapers, they all went along for the ride," as the lyrics state.[2] Carter spent 22 years in prison.

> **Argument One**
>
> The author now begins to present arguments: "'Hurricane' tells a story of the unjust treatment of an African-American man at the hands of the police, the courts, and the media, who punished him for a crime he did not commit."

Argument Two

The arguments in support of the thesis continue: "The message in 'Hurricane' is clear: Racism continues in the United States, and the color of one's skin can still trump the truth."

<u>The message in "Hurricane" is clear: Racism continues in the United States, and the color of one's skin can still trump the truth.</u> Carter's town of Paterson, New Jersey, had a history of racial profiling, so he was accustomed to being questioned by the police. As "Hurricane" states, "If you're black you might as well not show up on the street / 'Less you wanna draw the heat."[3] Carter's success in the boxing ring also made some of the local white people uneasy, and they were unhappy that he "is brave and gettin' braver," according to Dylan's lyrics.[4] These people were motivated by their racism to pin an awful crime on Carter. Even though no weapon was ever found to link Carter to the crime, the prosecution insisted he was guilty, with the lyrics stating, "And the all-white jury agreed."[5] Dylan made clear his opinion of the people who had conspired to frame Carter, stating, "Now all the criminals in their coats and their ties / Are free to drink martinis" while "Hurricane" did hard time.[6]

In addition to racially motivated crime, organized crime has been a problem in the United

Many people believed Rubin Carter was arrested and convicted based on insubstantial evidence.

States for decades. In major cities, many people have been forced to follow mob rules or face terrible consequences. People born into families connected with gangster activities have been

Argument Three

In the third argument, the author draws the reader in to connect with the main character of the song: "Dylan's 'Joey' conveys a tale of Joseph Gallo who, despite trying not to live a violent life, becomes active in the mob and becomes a victim of its violence."

expected to become active participants in the family "business." Dylan's "Joey" conveys a tale of Joseph Gallo who, despite trying not to live a violent life, becomes active in the mob and becomes a victim of its violence. Repeatedly called a "child of clay" in the lyrics, Gallo's life was molded by his surroundings, most notably the mob family he was born into.[7] Though he was known to have taken hostages at one point during a gang war, he struggled to resist the influences of those who, in his place, would kill the hostages. The lyrics quote him saying, "We're not those kind of men / It's peace and quiet that we need to go back to work again."[8] Gallo was willing to take part in some gang activity, but not murder. "Joey" tells the tale of a man caught in the middle. "The police department hounded him," and, because he did not always fit in with his family mob, his friends in prison "were black men 'cause they seemed to understand / What it's like to be in society with a shackle on your hand."[9]

Gallo was released from prison and, though he did not wish to be violent, he did want to get his standing back in his neighborhood. The lyrics in "Joey" state, "I have returned and now I want what's mine."[10] However, Dylan's lyrics spoke of a man who resisted violence: "in his later years he would not carry a gun," which was a dangerous

In "Hurricane" and "Joey," Dylan sang about the themes of racism, injustice, and violence.

choice for someone connected to the mob.[11] He was a man who did not want to kill, who would not go around armed, and who only wanted a good life for his family. However, in 1972, rival gangsters killed Gallo. The lyrics recurrently ask, "What made them want to come and blow you away?"[12]

History has been said to repeat itself. Because the worries expressed in the songs "Hurricane" and "Joey" have not been completely eliminated, these songs continue to carry important messages about the violent effects of racism, injustice, and violence. If the stories in these songs continue to be heard, people may learn from them and end violence and injustice in the future.

Conclusion

The last paragraph concludes the critique. It ties the preceding arguments together and repeats ideas from the thesis statement. The evidence presented in support of the arguments should make the conclusion logical and believable.

Thinking Critically about "Hurricane" and "Joey"

Now it is your turn to assess the critique. Consider these questions:

1. The thesis in this critique states that the songs "Hurricane" and "Joey" from *Desire* reflect concerns about violence and racism that existed during the 1960s. Are things better today? Why or why not?

2. What was the strongest argument made? The weakest? Were the arguments supported with examples from the lyrics?

3. Does the last sentence of the conclusion strengthen or weaken the overall argument? How else might you conclude the critique?

Other Approaches

What you have just read represents one way to interpret the songs "Hurricane" and "Joey" using historical criticism. Do you think there might be other ways to analyze these songs using the same theory? Recall that historical criticism places an artist and his or her work in the context of world events and developments of the time. What follow are two different ways that historical criticism could be applied to these two Dylan songs. The first contends these were bad people, and they got what they deserved. The second argues history repeats itself, and stories like these continue to unfold.

Undeserving of Sympathy

A historical critic could take the position that people like these two do not find themselves in trouble without somehow being the causes of that trouble. Whether they had done the actual bad deeds described in the songs or not, they had histories of criminal behavior. Perhaps they were treated worse than they should have been, and they were products of their respective social and historical contexts, but they were not guiltless. A thesis statement that could be used for this argument might be: Although Dylan tried to paint the protagonists of "Hurricane" and "Joey" as innocent victims of circumstance who were in the wrong places at the wrong times, both men had solid histories as violent criminals—a fact that Dylan overlooked when writing these songs.

Issues Still Exist

Examining the events described in "Hurricane" and "Joey," an author could point out that the underlying issues of racism, gang activities, corruption in the justice system, and so on have not been resolved. Bad things continue to happen in our society because underlying beliefs and prejudices that cause them have not truly changed. One possible thesis statement for this type of criticism could be: By recording in popular songs cases of the racism, violence, and injustice prevalent in the 1960s, Dylan provided a useful tool for modern society to measure its historical progress in those areas—and to find itself coming up short.

You Critique It

Now that you have learned about several critical theories and how to apply them to music, are you ready to perform your own critique? You have read that this type of evaluation can help you look at music in a new way and make you pay attention to certain issues you may not have otherwise recognized. So, why not use one of the critical theories profiled in this book to consider a fresh take on your favorite song?

First, choose a theory and the song you want to analyze. Remember that the theory is a springboard for asking questions about the work.

Next, write a specific question that relates to the theory you have selected. Then you can form your thesis, which should provide the answer to that question. Your thesis is the most important part of your critique and offers an argument about the work based on the tenets, or beliefs, of the theory you are applying. Recall that the thesis statement typically appears at the very end of the introductory paragraph of your essay. It is usually only one sentence long.

After you have written your thesis, find evidence to back it up. Good places to start are in the work itself or journals or articles that discuss what other people have said about it. Since you are critiquing a song, you may also want to read about the musician's life so you can get a sense of what factors may have affected the creative process. This can be especially useful if working within historical, biographical, or psychological criticism.

Depending on which theory you are applying, you can often find evidence in the song's lyrics and instrumentation. You also should explore parts of the song that seem to disprove your thesis and create an argument against them. As you do this, you might want to address what other critics have written about the song. Their quotes may help support your claim.

Before you start analyzing a work, think about the different arguments made in this book. Reflect on how evidence supporting the thesis was presented. Did you find that some of the techniques used to back up the arguments were more convincing than others? Try these methods as you prove your thesis in your own critique.

When you are finished writing your critique, read it over carefully. Is your thesis statement understandable? Do the supporting arguments flow logically, with the topic of each paragraph clearly stated? Can you add any information that would present your readers with a stronger argument in favor of your thesis? Were you able to use lyrics from the song, as well as quotations from other critics, to enhance your ideas?

Did you see the work in a new light?

Timeline

1959 Zimmerman begins performing in Minneapolis clubs.

1941 Bob Dylan is born Robert Allen Zimmerman on May 24 in Duluth, Minnesota.

1975 *Blood on the Tracks* is released.

1977 Dylan and Sara divorce.

1980 Dylan wins his first Grammy Award (best male rock vocal performance) on February 27 for "Gotta Serve Somebody."

1982 Dylan is inducted into the Songwriters' Hall of Fame.

1987 Dylan begins playing, touring, and recording with artists and bands, such as George Harrison and the Grateful Dead.

1988 Dylan is inducted into the Rock and Roll Hall of Fame.

1962 Zimmerman officially changes his name to Bob Dylan and releases his debut album, *Bob Dylan*.

1963 Dylan performs at the Newport Folk Festival in late July.

1964 Dylan releases two more important albums, *The Times They Are A-Changin'* and *Another Side of Bob Dylan*.

1965 Dylan plays electric, amplified music at the Newport Folk Festival and marries Sara Lownds.

1966 Dylan gets into a motorcycle accident in July.

1991 Dylan receives the Lifetime Achievement Award at the Grammys.

2008 Dylan receives a Special Citation Pulitzer Prize.

Glossary

acoustic
> Relating to a musical instrument that does not have an electronically modified sound.

angst
> A feeling of anxiety or insecurity.

apartheid
> The former policy of political and economic discrimination and racial segregation against blacks in South Africa.

cover
> A rendition of a song originally performed by another musician.

establishment
> A group of social, economic, and political leaders who form a sort of ruling class and control centers of power in society.

folk music
> A type of music that consists of stanzas, refrains, and simple melodies.

Grammys
> The Grammys, or Grammy Awards, are awards presented annually by the National Academy of Recording Arts and Sciences to acknowledge outstanding achievements in the music industry.

hallucinogenic
> Causing dreams, visions, and perceptions that are
> not real.

prolific
> Marked by a large output of creative or inventive
> activity.

symbolism
> Investing objects with meanings beyond their literal
> definitions.

zeitgeist
> General intellectual, moral, and cultural climate of
> an era.

Bibliography of Works and Criticism

Important Works

Bob Dylan, 1962

The Freewheelin' Bob Dylan, 1963

The Times They Are A-Changin', 1964

Another Side of Bob Dylan, 1964

Highway 61 Revisited, 1965

Blonde On Blonde, 1966

Bob Dylan's Greatest Hits, 1967

John Wesley Harding, 1967

Bob Dylan's Greatest Hits, Volume 2, 1971

Before The Flood, 1974

Blood On the Tracks, 1975

The Basement Tapes, 1975

Desire, 1976

Hard Rain, 1976

Saved, 1980

Empire Burlesque, 1985

The Bootleg Series Volumes 1-3, 1991

Bob Dylan's Greatest Hits Volume 3, 1994

Time Out of Mind, 1997

The Essential Bob Dylan, 2000

Critical Discussions

Corcoran, Neil. *Do You, Mr. Jones?: Bob Dylan with the Poets and Professors.* London: Random House, 2003. Print.

Marcus, Greil. *Invisible Republic: Bob Dylan's Basement Tapes.* New York: Henry Holt, 1997. Print.

Pichaske, David. *Song of the North Country: A Midwest Framework to the Songs of Bob Dylan.* London: Continuum, 2010. Print.

Sheehy, Colleen, ed. *Highway 61 Revisited: Bob Dylan's Road from Minnesota to the World.* Minneapolis, MN: U of Minnesota P, 2009. Print.

Resources

Selected Bibliography

Dylan, Bob. *The Essential Interviews*. Ed. Jonathan Cott. New York: Wenner, 2006. Print.

Dylan, Bob. *Lyrics: 1962–2001*. New York: Simon, 2004. Print.

Heylin, Clinton. *Bob Dylan: Behind the Shades Revisited*. New York: Harper, 2001. Print.

Sounes, Howard. *Down the Highway: The Life of Bob Dylan*. New York: Grove, 2001. Print.

Further Readings

Dylan, Bob. *Bob Dylan Revisited: 13 Graphic Interpretations of Bob Dylan's Songs*. New York: Norton, 2009.

Gilbert, Douglas, and David Marsh. *Forever Young: Photographs of Bob Dylan*. New York: Da Capo, 2006. Print.

Ricks, Christopher. *Dylan's Visions of Sin*. New York: Harper, 2003. Print.

Web Links

To learn more about critiquing the music of Bob Dylan, visit ABDO Publishing Company online at **www.abdopublishing.com**. Web sites about the music of Bob Dylan are featured on our Book Links page. These links are routinely monitored and updated to provide the most current information available.

For More Information

The Grammy Museum

800 West Olympic Boulevard, Los Angeles, CA 90015

213-765-6800

www.grammymuseum.org

The Grammy Museum contains four floors of interactive exhibits celebrating music and musicians of all genres.

Rock and Roll Hall of Fame and Museum

1100 Rock and Roll Boulevard, Cleveland, OH 44114

216-781-7625

www.rockhall.com

The Rock and Roll Hall of Fame and Museum is a nonprofit organization dedicated to educating people about the history and significance of rock and roll music. The museum hosts extensive content about Bob Dylan.

Source Notes

Chapter 1. Introduction to Critiques

None.

Chapter 2. A Closer Look at Bob Dylan

1. Howard Sounes. *Down the Highway: The Life of Bob Dylan*. New York: Grove, 2001. Print. 218.

Chapter 3. An Overview of Dylan's Protest Songs

1. Howard Sounes. *Down the Highway: The Life of Bob Dylan*. New York: Grove, 2001. Print. 122.

2. Clinton Heylin. *Bob Dylan: Behind the Shades Revisited*. New York: Harper, 2001. Print. 126.

3. Howard Sounes. *Down the Highway: The Life of Bob Dylan*. New York: Grove, 2001. Print. 122.

Chapter 4. How to Apply Social Criticism to Dylan's Protest Songs

1. Bob Dylan. *Lyrics: 1962–2001*. New York: Simon, 2004. Print. 81.

2. Ibid. 82.

3. Ibid.

4. Ibid. 53.

5. Ibid.

6. Ibid. 59–60.

7. Ibid. 60.

8. Ibid. 81.

Chapter 5. An Overview of Dylan's Personal Songs

1. Clinton Heylin. *Bob Dylan: Behind the Shades Revisited*. New York: Harper, 2001. Print. 154.

2. Bob Dylan. *Lyrics: 1962–2001*. New York: Simon, 2004. Print. 131.

3. Howard Sounes. *Down the Highway: The Life of Bob Dylan*. New York: Grove, 2001. Print. 186.

Chapter 6. How to Apply Biographical Criticism to Dylan's Personal Songs

1. Bob Dylan. *Lyrics: 1962–2001*. New York: Simon, 2004. Print. 131.

2. Ibid.

3. Ibid.

4. Ibid.

5. Ibid.

6. Ibid. 184.

7. Ibid.

8. Ibid. 185.

9. Ibid.

Chapter 7. An Overview of *Blood on the Tracks*

1. Clinton Heylin. *Bob Dylan: Behind the Shades Revisited*. New York: Harper, 2001. Print. 370.

Source Notes Continued

Chapter 8. How to Apply Feminist Criticism to *Blood on the Tracks*

1. Bob Dylan. *Lyrics: 1962–2001*. New York: Simon, 2004. Print. 331–332.

2. Bob Dylan. "If You See Her, Say Hello." *Bob Dylan*. Ram's Horn Music, n.d. Web. 22 Jan. 2011.

3. Bob Dylan. *Lyrics: 1962–2001*. New York: Simon, 2004. Print. 333.

4. Ibid. 336.

5. Ibid. 332.

6. Ibid.

7. Ibid.

8. Ibid. 336.

9. Ibid. 336–337.

Chapter 9. An Overview of "Hurricane" and "Joey" from *Desire*

1. Clinton Heylin. *Bob Dylan: Behind the Shades Revisited*. New York: Harper, 2001. Print. 399.

Chapter 10. How to Apply Historical Criticism to "Hurricane" and "Joey" from *Desire*

1. Bob Dylan. *Lyrics: 1962–2001*. New York: Simon, 2004. Print. 355.

2. Ibid. 357.

3. Ibid. 355.

4. Ibid. 356.

5. Ibid.

6. Ibid. 357.

7. Ibid. 363–364.

8. Ibid. 363.

9. Ibid. 364.

10. Ibid.

11. Ibid.

12. Ibid. 363–364.

Index

About the Author

Teresa Ryan Manzella is a freelance writer, editor, and musician living in Maplewood, Minnesota. Her written work covers a wide range of topics, including literary criticism.

Photo Credits

Harry Thompson/Getty Images, cover, 3; Photofest, 12, 19, 22, 25, 28, 40, 60, 66, 73, 91, 98; ABC/Photofest, 17; PBS/Photofest, 35; Michael Ochs Archives/Getty Images, 42, 63, 99 (bottom); Douglas R. Gilbert/Redferns/Getty Images, 44; AP Images, 46, 48, 55, 89, 99 (top); Columbia Records/Photofest, 78; Ed Bailey/AP Images, 81; Ray Stubblebine/AP Images, 84